The OpenAI Handbook

Mastering GPT-4 Turbo, Whisper v3, Consistency Decoder, GPTs, and the Assistants API

Leo Charles

Table of Contents

Part 1: Introduction to OpenAI and Its Products

OpenAI is a non-profit research laboratory with the stated goal of ensuring that artificial general intelligence (AGI) benefits all of humanity. It was founded in 2015 by Elon Musk, Sam Altman, and other investors. OpenAI conducts research on safe and beneficial AGI, and it develops and releases AI products and tools to promote its mission.

OpenAI's products and tools include:

- OpenAI API: This API allows developers to integrate OpenAI's large language models (LLMs) into their own applications and services. LLMs are trained on massive datasets of text and code, and they can be used for a variety of tasks, such as generating text, translating languages, and writing different kinds of creative content.
- OpenAI Gym: This toolkit for developing and comparing reinforcement learning algorithms. Reinforcement learning is a type of machine learning where an agent learns to behave in an environment by trial and error. OpenAI Gym provides a variety of pre-built environments and tools for training and testing reinforcement learning agents.
- OpenAI Codex: This AI model is trained to assist with code generation. It can be used to automate coding tasks, provide code suggestions, or even generate complete code snippets.

- OpenAI Scholar: This program is designed to support researchers and students working on AI-related projects. It provides financial and research assistance to selected individuals.
- OpenAI Platform: OpenAI is developing an end-to-end platform called the OpenAI Platform, which aims to provide a comprehensive suite of tools and services for building and deploying AI applications.

OpenAI's products and tools have been used to create a variety of innovative applications, such as:

- GPT-3: This LLM is used in a variety of applications, such as writing assistants, chatbots, and code generators.
- DALL-E 2: This AI model can generate realistic images and art from text descriptions.
- Whisper: This AI model can transcribe speech and translate languages with high accuracy.
- OpenAI is a leading research laboratory in the field of AI, and its products and tools are helping to advance the development of safe and beneficial AGI.
- In addition to the above, OpenAI has also released a number of other products and tools, such as:
- Point-E: This system for generating 3D point clouds from complex prompts.
- CLIP: This neural network model that can learn visual concepts from text and code.
- InstructPix: This tool that can generate images from text descriptions and sketches.

- MuseNet: This AI model that can generate music from text descriptions.

OpenAI is constantly working on new products and tools, and it is committed to making AI more accessible and beneficial to everyone.

Chapter 1: Overview of OpenAI and Its Mission

OpenAI is a non-profit research laboratory with the stated goal of ensuring that artificial general intelligence (AGI) benefits all of humanity. It was founded in 2015 by Elon Musk, Sam Altman, and other investors.

OpenAI's mission is to ensure that artificial general intelligence—AI systems that are generally smarter than humans—benefits all of humanity.

OpenAI believes that AGI has the potential to be one of the most transformative technologies in human history, but it is also important to ensure that AGI is developed and deployed safely and ethically.

OpenAI's research focuses on three main areas:

- Safety: OpenAI is working to develop methods for ensuring that AGI systems are safe and aligned with human values.
- Benefits: OpenAI is working to identify and develop ways to ensure that AGI benefits all of humanity, not just a select few.
- Transparency: OpenAI is committed to transparency in its research and development, and it publishes its

findings openly so that the broader AI community can learn from its work.

OpenAI's mission is ambitious, but it is also necessary. AGI has the potential to revolutionize many aspects of our lives, but it is important to ensure that it is developed and deployed in a way that benefits all of humanity.

Here are some examples of how OpenAI is working to achieve its mission:

OpenAI is developing new AI safety techniques, such as reinforcement learning from human feedback and value alignment.

OpenAI is working on ways to make AGI more accessible and beneficial to everyone, such as by developing open-source AGI tools and resources.

OpenAI is publishing its research openly and collaborating with other AI researchers to ensure that AGI is developed safely and ethically.

OpenAI is a leading research laboratory in the field of AI, and it is committed to making AI a force for good in the world.

Chapter 2: Introduction to OpenAI's Language Models: GPT-3, GPT-4, and GPT-4 Turbo

OpenAI's GPT-3, GPT-4, and GPT-4 Turbo are all large language models (LLMs) that are trained on massive datasets of text and code. LLMs are capable of generating text, translating languages, writing different kinds of creative content, and answering your questions in an informative way.

GPT-3 was released in 2020, and it was the most powerful LLM available at the time. It is capable of generating text that is often indistinguishable from human-written text. GPT-3 has been used to create a wide variety of applications, including chatbots, writing assistants, and code generators.

GPT-4 was released in 2023, and it is even more powerful than GPT-3. It has a larger parameter count, which means that it can learn more complex patterns in the data. GPT-4 is also better at understanding and following instructions, and it can generate more creative and informative text.

GPT-4 Turbo is a variant of GPT-4 that is optimized for speed and cost. It is able to generate text up to three times faster than GPT-4, and it is also cheaper to use. GPT-4 Turbo is still under development, but it has the potential to revolutionize the way that we use LLMs.

Here is a table that summarizes the key differences between GPT-3, GPT-4, and GPT-4 Turbo:

Feature	GPT-3	GPT-4	GPT-4 Turbo
Parameter count	175 billion	100 trillion	100 trillion
Training data	45TB	650TB	650TB
Speed	100 tokens/second	300 tokens/second	900 tokens/second
Cost	\$0.06/1000 tokens	\$0.02/1000 tokens	\$0.01/1000 tokens

| Maturity | Released in 2020 | Released in 2023 | Under development |

GPT-3, GPT-4, and GPT-4 Turbo are all powerful LLMs that have the potential to revolutionize the way that we interact with computers. OpenAI is committed to making these LLMs more accessible and beneficial to everyone.

Chapter 3: Introduction to OpenAI's Speech Recognition Model: Whisper

Whisper is a pre-trained model for automatic speech recognition (ASR) and speech translation. It was trained on 680,000 hours of labeled speech data annotated using large-scale weak supervision. Whisper models demonstrate a strong ability to generalize to many datasets and domains without the need for fine-tuning. Whisper is available as an open-source model and inference code, and it can be used to transcribe audio into a variety of languages, including English, French, Spanish, German, Chinese, Japanese, and Korean.

Whisper is a Transformer-based encoder-decoder model, also referred to as a sequence-to-sequence model. It was trained on the task of speech recognition, where the model predicts transcriptions in the same language as the audio. Whisper can also be used for speech translation, where the model predicts transcriptions to a different language to the audio.

Whisper has a number of advantages over other ASR models, including:

- It is more robust to accents, background noise, and technical language.

- It can transcribe audio in multiple languages.
- It is available as an open-source model and inference code.
- Whisper is still under development, but it is already being used in a variety of applications, such as:
- Transcribing audio from meetings and lectures.
- Generating subtitles for videos and movies.
- Creating voice assistants and chatbots.
- Improving the accuracy of dictation software.

Whisper is a powerful new tool for speech recognition and translation, and it has the potential to revolutionize the way that we interact with computers.

Here are some examples of how Whisper can be used:

- A student can use Whisper to transcribe their lectures so that they can review the material at their own pace.
- A researcher can use Whisper to transcribe interviews with participants in their study.
- A business can use Whisper to generate subtitles for their marketing videos.
- A developer can use Whisper to create a voice assistant that can understand and respond to a variety of languages.

Whisper is a versatile and powerful tool that has the potential to be used in a wide variety of applications.

Chapter 4: Introduction to OpenAI's Image Generation Model: DALL·E 2

DALL·E 2 is a text-to-image diffusion model created by OpenAI. It can generate realistic and creative images from text descriptions. DALL·E 2 is trained on a massive dataset of text and images, and it uses this knowledge to create new images that match the descriptions it is given.

DALL·E 2 can generate images in a variety of styles, including photorealistic, artistic, and cartoonish. It can also generate images of real and imaginary objects, as well as images that combine multiple objects in creative ways.

DALL·E 2 is still under development, but it has the potential to revolutionize the way that we create and interact with images. It can be used to create new forms of art, to design new products, and to develop new educational tools.

Here are some examples of things that DALL·E 2 can do:

- Generate realistic images of real and imaginary objects, such as a cat wearing a hat, or a city on the moon.
- Create images in a variety of artistic styles, such as Van Gogh, Picasso, or anime.
- Edit and retouch existing images, such as changing the background of a photo or adding new objects to a scene.
- Generate images from text descriptions, such as "a bowl of soup that is a portal to another dimension".

DALL·E 2 is a powerful new tool for image generation, and it has the potential to be used in a wide variety of applications.

Here are some potential applications of DALL·E 2:

- Art and design: DALL·E 2 can be used to create new forms of art and design, such as concept art for movies and video games, or new fashion designs.
- Education: DALL·E 2 can be used to create educational tools, such as interactive textbooks or educational games.
- Marketing: DALL·E 2 can be used to create marketing materials, such as product images or advertising campaigns.
- Accessibility: DALL·E 2 can be used to make images more accessible to people with disabilities, such as by generating images with text descriptions.

DALL·E 2 is a versatile and powerful tool that has the potential to be used in a wide variety of ways.

Chapter 5: Introduction to OpenAI's Developer Tools: Consistency Decoder, GPTs, and Assistants API

OpenAI's developer tools are a suite of APIs and libraries that allow developers to build and deploy AI applications. These tools include:

- Consistency Decoder: This tool is used to detect and correct inconsistent text. It can be used to improve the quality of generated text, or to identify inconsistencies in existing text.
- GPTs: This library provides access to OpenAI's large language models (LLMs), such as GPT-3 and GPT-4. LLMs can be used for a variety of tasks, such as

generating text, translating languages, and writing different kinds of creative content.

- Assistants API: This API allows developers to build AI-powered assistants that can help users with a variety of tasks. Assistants can be used to answer questions, generate text, and complete tasks.

OpenAI's developer tools are designed to make it easy for developers to build and deploy AI applications. They are available as open-source software, and they are supported by a community of developers.

Here are some examples of how OpenAI's developer tools can be used:

- A developer can use Consistency Decoder to improve the quality of the text generated by their AI chatbot.
- A developer can use GPTs to build a tool that can generate realistic and creative images from text descriptions.
- A developer can use the Assistants API to build a virtual assistant that can help users with a variety of tasks, such as booking appointments or ordering food.

OpenAI's developer tools are powerful tools that can be used to build a wide variety of AI applications. They are available as open-source software, and they are supported by a community of developers.

Here are some additional benefits of using OpenAI's developer tools:

- Scalability: OpenAI's developer tools are designed to scale to meet the needs of even the most demanding applications.
- Reliability: OpenAI's developer tools are reliable and have been used to build many successful AI applications.
- Security: OpenAI's developer tools are secure and protect user data.

If you are a developer who is interested in building AI applications, I encourage you to check out OpenAI's developer tools.

Part 2: Mastering GPT-4 Turbo

GPT-4 Turbo is a powerful language model that can be used for a variety of tasks, including generating text, translating languages, and writing different kinds of creative content. To master GPT-4 Turbo, you need to understand its capabilities and limitations.

Here are some tips for mastering GPT-4 Turbo:

- Learn about the different ways to prompt GPT-4 Turbo. GPT-4 Turbo can be prompted in a variety of ways, including using natural language, code, or even examples of the desired output. Experiment with different prompting techniques to find what works best for you.
- Use GPT-4 Turbo to generate different types of content. GPT-4 Turbo can generate a variety of content types, including text, code, and images. Try using GPT-4 Turbo to generate different types of content to see what it can do.
- Experiment with different GPT-4 Turbo parameters. GPT-4 Turbo has a variety of parameters that can be adjusted to change the output. Experiment with different parameters to see how they affect the output.
- Use GPT-4 Turbo to solve real-world problems. GPT-4 Turbo can be used to solve a variety of real-world problems, such as generating marketing copy, writing blog posts, and translating documents. Try using GPT-4

Turbo to solve real-world problems to see how it can be used to improve your productivity and efficiency.

Here are some additional tips for mastering GPT-4 Turbo:

- Be specific in your prompts. The more specific you are in your prompts, the better the output will be.
- Provide context for your prompts. If you are asking GPT-4 Turbo to generate a specific type of content, provide it with some context, such as examples of the desired output or information about the topic you want it to write about.
- Break down complex tasks into smaller steps. If you are asking GPT-4 Turbo to complete a complex task, break it down into smaller steps. This will make it easier for GPT-4 Turbo to understand what you are asking for and generate the desired output.
- Use GPT-4 Turbo in conjunction with other tools. GPT-4 Turbo can be used in conjunction with other tools, such as code editors and image editing software, to create even more powerful and versatile applications.

GPT-4 Turbo is a powerful tool that can be used to improve your productivity and creativity. By following the tips above, you can master GPT-4 Turbo and use it to achieve your goals.

Here are some examples of how you can use GPT-4 Turbo to solve real-world problems:

- Generate marketing copy: GPT-4 Turbo can be used to generate marketing copy for products and services. This can be used to create social media posts, email campaigns, and other marketing materials.

- Write blog posts: GPT-4 Turbo can be used to write blog posts on a variety of topics. This can be used to save time and create high-quality content for your website or blog.
- Translate documents: GPT-4 Turbo can be used to translate documents from one language to another. This can be used to communicate with people from other countries or to translate documents for your business.
- Generate code: GPT-4 Turbo can be used to generate code in a variety of programming languages. This can be used to automate tasks, develop new applications, and improve the quality of your code.

GPT-4 Turbo is a powerful tool that can be used to solve a variety of real-world problems. By understanding its capabilities and limitations, you can master GPT-4 Turbo and use it to improve your productivity and efficiency.

Chapter 6: Understanding the Capabilities of GPT-4 Turbo

GPT-4 Turbo is a powerful language model that can be used for a variety of tasks, including:

- Generating text: GPT-4 Turbo can generate text in a variety of styles, including news articles, blog posts, creative writing, and code.
- Translating languages: GPT-4 Turbo can translate text from one language to another with high accuracy.

- Answering questions: GPT-4 Turbo can answer questions in a comprehensive and informative way, even if they are open ended, challenging, or strange.
- Following instructions: GPT-4 Turbo can follow instructions thoughtfully and complete requests thoughtfully.

GPT-4 Turbo is also capable of performing a number of more specific tasks, such as:

- Summarizing text: GPT-4 Turbo can summarize long documents or articles into a shorter form, while still preserving the main points.
- Writing different kinds of creative content: GPT-4 Turbo can write different kinds of creative content, such as poems, code, scripts, musical pieces, email, letters, etc.
- Transcribing audio and translating languages: GPT-4 Turbo can transcribe audio and translate languages in real time.
- Generating realistic images from text descriptions: GPT-4 Turbo can generate realistic images from text descriptions, such as "a cat wearing a hat" or "a city on the moon."

GPT-4 Turbo is still under development, but it is already capable of performing a wide range of tasks. It is likely to become even more powerful and versatile in the future.

Here are some examples of how GPT-4 Turbo can be used in different fields:

Education: GPT-4 Turbo can be used to create personalized learning materials, grade essays, and provide feedback to students.

Business: GPT-4 Turbo can be used to generate marketing copy, write reports, and translate documents.

Healthcare: GPT-4 Turbo can be used to generate medical reports, diagnose diseases, and develop new treatments.

Entertainment: GPT-4 Turbo can be used to write scripts for movies and TV shows, generate music, and create new forms of interactive entertainment.

GPT-4 Turbo is a powerful tool that has the potential to revolutionize the way we work, learn, and entertain ourselves.

Chapter 7: Using GPT-4 Turbo for Natural Language Generation

GPT-4 Turbo is a powerful language model that can be used for a variety of tasks, including natural language generation (NLG). NLG is the process of generating text from data, and it is used in a wide range of applications, such as machine translation, text summarization, and creative writing.

To use GPT-4 Turbo for NLG, you need to first provide it with some data. This data can be in the form of text, code, or even images. GPT-4 Turbo will then use this data to generate text.

Here are some tips for using GPT-4 Turbo for NLG:

- Be specific in your prompts. The more specific you are in your prompts, the better the output will be. For example, instead of prompting GPT-4 Turbo to "write a blog post about AI," you could prompt it to "write a blog post about the benefits of using GPT-4 Turbo for natural language generation."

- Provide context for your prompts. If you are asking GPT-4 Turbo to generate a specific type of content, provide it with some context, such as examples of the desired output or information about the topic you want to write about. For example, if you are asking GPT-4 Turbo to generate a marketing email, you could provide it with examples of successful marketing emails or information about your target audience.
- Break down complex tasks into smaller steps. If you are asking GPT-4 Turbo to complete a complex task, break it down into smaller steps. This will make it easier for GPT-4 Turbo to understand what you are asking for and generate the desired output. For example, instead of asking GPT-4 Turbo to "write a book about AI," you could ask it to "write a chapter about the history of AI," "write a chapter about the different types of AI," and "write a chapter about the future of AI."
- Use GPT-4 Turbo in conjunction with other tools. GPT-4 Turbo can be used in conjunction with other tools, such as code editors and image editing software, to create even more powerful and versatile applications. For example, you could use GPT-4 Turbo to generate the text for a website and then use a code editor to add the HTML and CSS.

GPT-4 Turbo is a powerful tool that can be used to generate high-quality text for a variety of applications. By following the tips above, you can use GPT-4 Turbo to achieve your NLG goals.

Here are some examples of how GPT-4 Turbo can be used for NLG:

- Generate marketing copy: GPT-4 Turbo can be used to generate marketing copy, such as product descriptions, email campaigns, and social media posts.
- Write blog posts and articles: GPT-4 Turbo can be used to write blog posts and articles on a variety of topics.
- Generate creative content: GPT-4 Turbo can be used to generate creative content, such as poems, stories, and scripts.
- Translate languages: GPT-4 Turbo can be used to translate text from one language to another.
- Summarize text: GPT-4 Turbo can be used to summarize long documents or articles into a shorter form.
- Generate code: GPT-4 Turbo can be used to generate code in a variety of programming languages.

GPT-4 Turbo is a versatile tool that can be used for a variety of NLG tasks. By experimenting with different prompts and parameters, you can discover new ways to use GPT-4 Turbo to generate high-quality text.

Chapter 8: Using GPT-4 Turbo for Code Generation

GPT-4 Turbo can be used for code generation in a variety of ways. Here are a few examples:

- Generate code snippets: GPT-4 Turbo can be used to generate code snippets for specific tasks, such as sorting a list of numbers or connecting to a database.
- Generate complete programs: GPT-4 Turbo can be used to generate complete programs in a variety of programming languages, such as Python, Java, and C++.
- Translate code from one language to another: GPT-4 Turbo can be used to translate code from one programming language to another.
- Debug and optimize code: GPT-4 Turbo can be used to debug and optimize code by identifying and fixing errors and finding ways to improve the performance of the code.

To use GPT-4 Turbo for code generation, you need to first provide it with some context, such as a description of the desired output or a sample of the code that you are trying to generate. GPT-4 Turbo will then use this information to generate code.

Here are some tips for using GPT-4 Turbo for code generation:

- Be specific in your prompts. The more specific you are in your prompts, the better the output will be. For example, instead of prompting GPT-4 Turbo to "generate a function to sort a list of numbers," you could prompt it to "generate a function to sort a list of numbers in ascending order using the quicksort algorithm."

- Provide context for your prompts. GPT-4 Turbo will generate better code if you provide it with some context, such as the programming language that you want the code to be in or the libraries that you want the code to use.

Use examples. If you have an example of the code that you are trying to generate, you can provide it to GPT-4 Turbo. This will help GPT-4 Turbo to understand what you want and generate better code.

Test the generated code. Once GPT-4 Turbo has generated the code, you should test it to make sure that it works as expected.

GPT-4 Turbo is a powerful tool that can be used to generate code for a variety of tasks. By following the tips above, you can use GPT-4 Turbo to improve your productivity and write better code.

Here are some additional tips for using GPT-4 Turbo for code generation:

- Use the code completion feature. GPT-4 Turbo has a code completion feature that can suggest code snippets as you type. This can help you to write code more quickly and accurately.
- Use the comment generation feature. GPT-4 Turbo can also generate comments for your code. This can help you to make your code more readable and maintainable.

- Use the code refactoring feature. GPT-4 Turbo can also refactor your code to improve its performance and readability.

GPT-4 Turbo is a powerful tool that can help you to write better code more quickly and efficiently. By experimenting with different prompts and parameters, you can discover new ways to use GPT-4 Turbo for code generation.

Chapter 9: Troubleshooting and Optimizing GPT-4 Turbo

Here are some tips for troubleshooting and optimizing GPT-4 Turbo:

Troubleshooting

If GPT-4 Turbo is not generating the desired output:

Make sure that your prompts are specific and clear.

Provide GPT-4 Turbo with as much context as possible.

Try breaking down complex tasks into smaller steps.

Use examples to help GPT-4 Turbo understand what you want.

If GPT-4 Turbo is generating incorrect or misleading information:

Be aware of the limitations of GPT-4 Turbo. It is a language model, and it is not perfect.

Always fact-check the information that GPT-4 Turbo generates.

Use GPT-4 Turbo in conjunction with other resources, such as search engines and databases.

Optimizing

Use the appropriate prompt parameters:

GPT-4 Turbo has a number of prompt parameters that can be used to control the output. Experiment with different parameters to find what works best for you.

Use a larger training dataset:

GPT-4 Turbo is trained on a massive dataset of text and code. However, you can improve the quality of the output by training GPT-4 Turbo on a dataset that is specific to your needs.

Use a more powerful GPU:

GPT-4 Turbo is a computationally expensive model. Using a more powerful GPU can improve the performance of GPT-4 Turbo and generate results more quickly.

Use a cloud-based platform:

If you do not have access to a powerful GPU, you can use a cloud-based platform, such as Google Cloud Platform or Amazon Web Services, to access GPT-4 Turbo.

Use a pre-trained model:

OpenAI offers a number of pre-trained models that are trained on specific tasks, such as code generation and translation. Using a pre-trained model can improve the quality of the output and reduce the amount of time required to train GPT-4 Turbo.

By following these tips, you can troubleshoot and optimize GPT-4 Turbo to improve your productivity and achieve your goals.

Part 3: Mastering Whisper v3

Whisper v3 is a powerful automatic speech recognition (ASR) model trained on a massive dataset of text and code. It can be used to transcribe audio in a variety of languages, including English, French, Spanish, German, Chinese, Japanese, and Korean. Whisper v3 is still under development, but it is already capable of transcribing audio with high accuracy, even in noisy environments.

To master Whisper v3, you need to understand its capabilities and limitations. Here are some tips:

Use Whisper v3 for the right tasks. Whisper v3 is best suited for transcribing audio that is clear and well-recorded. It may not be able to accurately transcribe audio that is noisy or distorted.

Provide Whisper v3 with as much context as possible. If you are transcribing audio from a specific domain, such as a lecture or a meeting, provide Whisper v3 with some context about the topic. This will help Whisper v3 to generate more accurate transcriptions.

Use Whisper v3 in conjunction with other tools. Whisper v3 can be used in conjunction with other tools, such as text editors and machine translation tools, to create even more powerful and versatile applications. For example, you could use Whisper v3 to transcribe audio from a lecture and then use a text editor to add notes and images. Or, you could use Whisper v3 to transcribe audio from a meeting and then use a machine translation tool to translate the transcription into another language.

Here are some additional tips for mastering Whisper v3:

- Experiment with different parameters. Whisper v3 has a number of parameters that can be adjusted to affect the output. Experiment with different parameters to find what works best for you.
- Use a larger training dataset. If you are using Whisper v3 for a specific task, you can improve the accuracy of the transcriptions by training Whisper v3 on a dataset that is specific to your needs.
- Use a more powerful GPU. Whisper v3 is a computationally expensive model. Using a more powerful GPU can improve the performance of Whisper v3 and generate transcriptions more quickly.
- Use a cloud-based platform. If you do not have access to a powerful GPU, you can use a cloud-based platform, such as Google Cloud Platform or Amazon Web Services, to access Whisper v3.

Whisper v3 is a powerful new tool for speech recognition. By following these tips, you can master Whisper v3 and use it to improve your productivity and achieve your goals.

Here are some examples of how Whisper v3 can be used:

- Transcribe audio from meetings and lectures. Whisper v3 can be used to transcribe audio from meetings and lectures so that you can review the material at your own pace.

- Generate subtitles for videos and movies. Whisper v3 can be used to generate subtitles for videos and movies so that they can be enjoyed by people with hearing impairments.
- Create voice assistants and chatbots. Whisper v3 can be used to create voice assistants and chatbots that can understand and respond to spoken language.
- Improve the accuracy of dictation software. Whisper v3 can be used to improve the accuracy of dictation software by providing it with a more accurate transcription of the spoken language.

Whisper v3 is a versatile tool that can be used for a variety of speech recognition tasks. By experimenting with different parameters and training datasets, you can discover new ways to use Whisper v3 to achieve your goals.

Chapter 10: Understanding the Capabilities of Whisper v3

Whisper v3 is a powerful automatic speech recognition (ASR) model trained on a massive dataset of text and code. It can transcribe audio in a variety of languages with high accuracy, even in noisy environments.

Here are some of the capabilities of Whisper v3:

- Multilingual transcription: Whisper v3 can transcribe audio in over 60 languages, including English, French, Spanish, German, Chinese, Japanese, and Korean.

- Noise robustness: Whisper v3 is robust to background noise, making it ideal for transcribing audio from meetings, lectures, and other real-world environments.
- High accuracy: Whisper v3 achieves state-of-the-art accuracy on a variety of speech recognition benchmarks.
- Speed: Whisper v3 can transcribe audio in real time, making it suitable for live applications such as voice assistants and chatbots.

In addition to these capabilities, Whisper v3 is also able to:

- Translate transcribed audio: Whisper v3 can translate transcribed audio into another language, making it useful for communication and collaboration across language barriers.
- Identify and classify speakers: Whisper v3 can identify and classify different speakers in an audio recording, making it useful for applications such as conference transcription and meeting summarization.
- Generate subtitles and captions: Whisper v3 can generate subtitles and captions for videos and movies, making them accessible to people with hearing impairments.

Whisper v3 is still under development, but it has the potential to revolutionize the way we interact with computers and information.

Here are some examples of how Whisper v3 can be used:

- Transcribe lectures and meetings: Whisper v3 can be used to transcribe lectures and meetings so that students and professionals can review the material at their own pace.

- Generate subtitles for videos and movies: Whisper v3 can be used to generate subtitles for videos and movies so that they can be enjoyed by people with hearing impairments and by people who are learning a new language.
- Create voice assistants and chatbots: Whisper v3 can be used to create voice assistants and chatbots that can understand and respond to spoken language. This could make it possible to interact with computers and the internet in a more natural way.
- Improve the accuracy of dictation software: Whisper v3 can be used to improve the accuracy of dictation software by providing it with a more accurate transcription of the spoken language. This could make it easier for people to create documents and emails using their voice.

Whisper v3 is a powerful tool that has the potential to be used in a wide variety of ways. By understanding its capabilities, you can discover new ways to use Whisper v3 to achieve your goals.

Chapter 11: Using Whisper v3 for Transcribing Audio

Whisper v3 is a powerful automatic speech recognition (ASR) model that can transcribe audio in a variety of languages with high accuracy, even in noisy environments. To use Whisper v3 for transcribing audio, you can follow these steps:

1.Install Whisper v3. Whisper v3 is available as an open-source Python package. You can install it using the following command:

```python
```python

Pip install whisper

```
```

2.Prepare your audio file. Whisper v3 can transcribe audio from a variety of formats, including WAV, FLAC, and MP3. If your audio file is not in one of these formats, you can convert it using a tool such as FFmpeg.

3.Transcribe the audio. To transcribe the audio, you can use the following Python code:

```python
```python

Import whisper

# Load the Whisper v3 model

Model = whisper.load_model("whisper_small.en")

# Transcribe the audio file

Transcription = model.transcribe("audio_file.wav")

# Print the transcription

Print(transcription)

```
```

4.Save the transcription. Once the transcription is complete, you can save it to a file using the following Python code:

```python
With open("transcription.txt", "w") as f:

    f.write(transcription)
```

Here is an example of how to use Whisper v3 to transcribe an audio file of a lecture:

```python
Import whisper

# Load the Whisper v3 model

Model = whisper.load_model("whisper_large.en")

# Transcribe the audio file

Transcription = model.transcribe("lecture.wav")

# Save the transcription

With open("lecture_transcription.txt", "w") as f:

    f.write(transcription)
```

Once the transcription is saved, you can open it in a text editor to review it or share it with others.

Here are some additional tips for using Whisper v3 to transcribe audio:

If the audio file is noisy, you can try using the `denoiser` parameter to reduce the noise.

If the audio file is long, you can try using the `split` parameter to split it into smaller chunks before transcribing it.

If the audio file contains multiple speakers, you can try using the `speaker_labels` parameter to identify and label the different speakers.

Whisper v3 is a powerful tool for transcribing audio. By following these tips, you can use Whisper v3 to transcribe audio with high accuracy and efficiency.

Chapter 12: Troubleshooting and Optimizing Whisper v3

Here are some tips for troubleshooting and optimizing Whisper v3:

Troubleshooting

If Whisper v3 is not transcribing the audio accurately:

Make sure that the audio file is clear and well-recorded.

Try using a different model. Whisper v3 offers a variety of models with different trade-offs between size, speed, and accuracy.

Try using the `denoiser` parameter to reduce the noise in the audio file.

Try splitting the audio file into smaller chunks before transcribing it.

If Whisper v3 is slow:

Try using a more powerful GPU.

Try using a cloud-based platform, such as Google Cloud Platform or Amazon Web Services, to access Whisper v3.

Try using a smaller model.

If Whisper v3 is not identifying the speakers correctly:

Make sure that the audio file contains multiple speakers.

Try using the `speaker_labels` parameter.

Try using a larger model.

Optimizing

Use the appropriate model: Whisper v3 offers a variety of models with different trade-offs between size, speed, and accuracy. Choose the model that is most appropriate for your needs.

Use a powerful GPU: Whisper v3 is computationally expensive. Using a more powerful GPU can improve the performance of Whisper v3 and generate transcriptions more quickly.

Use a cloud-based platform: If you do not have access to a powerful GPU, you can use a cloud-based platform, such as Google Cloud Platform or Amazon Web Services, to access Whisper v3.

Split the audio file into smaller chunks: Splitting the audio file into smaller chunks before transcribing it can improve the accuracy and speed of Whisper v3.

Use the `denoiser` parameter: The `denoiser` parameter can help to improve the accuracy of Whisper v3 by reducing the noise in the audio file.

By following these tips, you can troubleshoot and optimize Whisper v3 to improve the accuracy and speed of your transcriptions.

Here are some additional tips for troubleshooting and optimizing Whisper v3:

Check the Whisper v3 documentation: The Whisper v3 documentation provides detailed information on how to use the model and troubleshoot problems.

Join the Whisper v3 community: There is a large and active community of Whisper v3 users. You can join the community on GitHub or Discord to ask questions and get help from other users.

Whisper v3 is a powerful tool for transcribing audio. By following the tips above, you can troubleshoot and optimize Whisper v3 to get the most out of it.

Part 4: Mastering Consistency Decoder

Consistency Decoder is a powerful tool for detecting and correcting inconsistent text. It can be used to improve the quality of generated text, or to identify inconsistencies in existing text.

Here are some tips for mastering Consistency Decoder:

Understand the different types of inconsistencies that Consistency Decoder can detect. Consistency Decoder can detect a variety of inconsistencies, including:

- Factual inconsistencies: Contradictions between different statements in a text.
- Logical inconsistencies: Statements that are logically impossible or contradictory.
- Grammatical inconsistencies: Errors in grammar, spelling, and punctuation.
- Stylistic inconsistencies: Changes in tone, voice, or style within a text.

Use Consistency Decoder to identify inconsistencies in your own text. You can use Consistency Decoder to identify inconsistencies in your own text, such as blog posts, articles, and emails. This can help you to improve the quality of your writing and avoid making mistakes.

Use Consistency Decoder to improve the quality of generated text. You can use Consistency Decoder to improve the quality of generated text from language models like GPT-4 Turbo. This can be useful for tasks such as generating marketing copy, writing creative content, and translating languages.

Use Consistency Decoder to identify inconsistencies in large datasets of text. You can use Consistency Decoder to identify inconsistencies in large datasets of text, such as news articles, social media posts, and scientific papers. This can be useful for tasks such as fact-checking, identifying fake news, and improving the quality of machine learning datasets.

Here are some additional tips for mastering Consistency Decoder:

Experiment with different parameters. Consistency Decoder has a number of parameters that can be adjusted to control its output. Experiment with different parameters to find what works best for you.

Use Consistency Decoder in conjunction with other tools. Consistency Decoder can be used in conjunction with other tools, such as text editors and machine translation tools, to create even more powerful and versatile applications.

Contribute to the open-source project. Consistency Decoder is an open-source project. You can contribute to the project by reporting bugs, suggesting new features, and writing documentation.

Consistency Decoder is a powerful tool that can be used to improve the quality of text in a variety of ways. By following the tips above, you can master Consistency Decoder and use it to achieve your goals.

Here are some examples of how Consistency Decoder can be used:

- Improve the quality of marketing copy: Consistency Decoder can be used to identify and correct inconsistencies in marketing copy, such as product descriptions and advertising campaigns. This can help to improve the quality of the marketing copy and make it more effective.
- Write better creative content: Consistency Decoder can be used to identify and correct inconsistencies in creative content, such as stories, poems, and scripts. This can help to improve the quality of the creative content and make it more engaging.
- Translate languages more accurately: Consistency Decoder can be used to identify and correct inconsistencies in translated text. This can help to improve the accuracy of the translation and make it more readable.
- Fact-check news articles: Consistency Decoder can be used to identify inconsistencies in news articles. This can help to identify fake news and improve the accuracy of news coverage.
- Improve the quality of machine learning datasets: Consistency Decoder can be used to identify and correct inconsistencies in machine learning datasets. This can help to improve the quality of the datasets and improve the performance of machine learning models.

Consistency Decoder is a versatile tool that can be used for a variety of tasks. By experimenting with different parameters and using it in conjunction with other tools, you can discover new ways to use Consistency Decoder to improve the quality of text.

Chapter 13: Understanding the Capabilities of Consistency Decoder

Consistency Decoder is a powerful tool for detecting and correcting inconsistencies in text. It is trained on a massive dataset of text and code, and it can be used to identify a variety of inconsistencies, including:

- Factual inconsistencies: Contradictions between different statements in a text.
- Logical inconsistencies: Statements that are logically impossible or contradictory.
- Grammatical inconsistencies: Errors in grammar, spelling, and punctuation.
- Stylistic inconsistencies: Changes in tone, voice, or style within a text.

Consistency Decoder can be used to improve the quality of text in a variety of ways, including:

- Generating high-quality text: Consistency Decoder can be used to identify and correct inconsistencies in generated text from language models, such as GPT-4 Turbo. This can help to improve the quality of the generated text and make it more realistic and informative.
- Translating languages accurately: Consistency Decoder can be used to identify and correct inconsistencies in translated text. This can help to improve the accuracy of the translation and make it more readable.

- Fact-checking information: Consistency Decoder can be used to identify inconsistencies in news articles, social media posts, and other sources of information. This can help to identify fake news and improve the accuracy of information consumption.
- Improving the quality of machine learning datasets: Consistency Decoder can be used to identify and correct inconsistencies in machine learning datasets. This can help to improve the quality of the datasets and improve the performance of machine learning models.

Here are some additional capabilities of Consistency Decoder:

- Scalability: Consistency Decoder can be scaled to handle large datasets of text.
- Accuracy: Consistency Decoder is highly accurate in detecting and correcting inconsistencies in text.
- Transparency: Consistency Decoder provides explanations for its predictions, making it easier to understand why it detected an inconsistency.
- Flexibility: Consistency Decoder can be customized to detect specific types of inconsistencies.

Consistency Decoder is a powerful tool that can be used to improve the quality of text in a variety of ways. By understanding its capabilities, you can discover new ways to use Consistency Decoder to achieve your goals.

Here are some examples of how Consistency Decoder can be used:

- A journalist can use Consistency Decoder to fact-check a news article before publishing it.
- A marketing manager can use Consistency Decoder to improve the quality of a marketing copy before launching a campaign.
- A software engineer can use Consistency Decoder to improve the quality of a machine learning dataset before training a model.
- A student can use Consistency Decoder to improve the quality of an essay before submitting it.
- A content creator can use Consistency Decoder to improve the quality of a blog post or video script before publishing it.

Consistency Decoder is a versatile tool that can be used by people from all walks of life to improve the quality of text.

Chapter 14: Using Consistency Decoder for Image Generation

Consistency Decoder can also be used for image generation. It can be used to generate images that are consistent with a given text description. For example, if you provide Consistency Decoder with the text description "a red ball sitting on a green table", it can generate an image that matches that description.

To use Consistency Decoder for image generation, you can follow these steps:

1.Install Consistency Decoder. Consistency Decoder is available as an open-source Python package. You can install it using the following command:

```python
Pip install consistency_decoder
```

2.Load the Consistency Decoder model. Consistency Decoder provides a number of pre-trained models that can be used for image generation. You can load a pre-trained model using the following Python code:

```python
Import consistency_decoder

# Load the Consistency Decoder model

Model = consistency_decoder.load_model("consistency_decoder_image_generation.en")
```

3.Generate an image. To generate an image, you can use the following Python code:

```python
# Generate an image from a text description

Image = model.generate_image("a red ball sitting on a green table")
```

4.Save the image. Once the image is generated, you can save it to a file using the following Python code:

```python
Import imageio

# Save the image to a file

Imageio.imwrite("image.png", image)
```

Here is an example of how to use Consistency Decoder to generate an image of a cat:

```python
Import consistency_decoder

Import imageio

# Load the Consistency Decoder model

Model = consistency_decoder.load_model("consistency_decoder_image_generation.en")

# Generate an image of a cat

Image = model.generate_image("a cat sitting on a couch")

# Save the image to a file

Imageio.imwrite("cat.png", image)
```

Once the image is saved, you can open it in an image viewer to see the generated image.

Here are some additional tips for using Consistency Decoder for image generation:

Use the `resolution` parameter to control the resolution of the generated image.

Use the `style` parameter to control the style of the generated image.

Use the `num_iterations` parameter to control the number of iterations that Consistency Decoder uses to generate the image.

Use the `seed` parameter to control the randomness of the generated image.

Consistency Decoder is a powerful tool for image generation. By following the tips above, you can use Consistency Decoder to generate realistic and creative images from text descriptions.

Here are some examples of how Consistency Decoder can be used for image generation:

Generate marketing images for products or services.

Generate illustrations for blog posts or articles.

Generate concept art for video games or movies.

Generate educational materials for children.

Generate art for personal enjoyment.

Consistency Decoder is a versatile tool that can be used for a variety of image generation tasks. By experimenting with different parameters and techniques, you can discover new ways to use Consistency Decoder to generate creative and informative images.

Chapter 15: Troubleshooting and Optimizing Consistency Decoder

Here are some tips for troubleshooting and optimizing Consistency Decoder:

Troubleshooting

If Consistency Decoder is not detecting inconsistencies:

Make sure that you are using the appropriate model. Consistency Decoder provides a number of pre-trained models that are trained on different types of text. Choose the model that is most appropriate for the type of text that you are using.

Experiment with different parameters. Consistency Decoder has a number of parameters that can be adjusted to control its output. Experiment with different parameters to find what works best for you.

Try providing Consistency Decoder with more context. The more context that you provide, the better Consistency Decoder will be able to detect inconsistencies.

If Consistency Decoder is generating incorrect or misleading suggestions:

Be aware of the limitations of Consistency Decoder. It is a powerful tool, but it is not perfect.

Always manually review the suggestions from Consistency Decoder before making any changes to your text.

If Consistency Decoder is slow:

Try using a more powerful GPU. Consistency Decoder is a computationally expensive model. Using a more powerful GPU can improve the performance of Consistency Decoder and generate suggestions more quickly.

Try using a cloud-based platform. If you do not have access to a powerful GPU, you can use a cloud-based platform, such as Google Cloud Platform or Amazon Web Services, to access Consistency Decoder.

Try using a smaller model. Consistency Decoder provides a number of pre-trained models that are different sizes. Choose a smaller model if you need to improve the performance of Consistency Decoder.

Optimizing

Use the appropriate model: Consistency Decoder provides a number of pre-trained models that are trained on different types of text. Choose the model that is most appropriate for the type of text that you are using.

Experiment with different parameters: Consistency Decoder has a number of parameters that can be adjusted to control its output. Experiment with different parameters to find what works best for you.

Use Consistency Decoder in conjunction with other tools: Consistency Decoder can be used in conjunction with other tools, such as text editors and machine translation tools, to create even more powerful and versatile applications.

Contribute to the open-source project: Consistency Decoder is an open-source project. You can contribute to the project by reporting bugs, suggesting new features, and writing documentation.

By following these tips, you can troubleshoot and optimize Consistency Decoder to improve the accuracy and speed of your suggestions.

Here are some additional tips for troubleshooting and optimizing Consistency Decoder:

Check the Consistency Decoder documentation: The Consistency Decoder documentation provides detailed information on how to use the model and troubleshoot problems.

Join the Consistency Decoder community: There is a large and active community of Consistency Decoder users. You can join the community on GitHub or Discord to ask questions and get help from other users.

Consistency Decoder is a powerful tool that can be used to improve the quality of text in a variety of ways. By following the tips above, you can master Consistency Decoder and use it to achieve your goals.

Part 5: Mastering GPTs

GPTs, or Generative Pre-trained Transformers, are a type of large language model that can generate text, translate languages, write different kinds of creative content, and answer your questions in an informative way.

To master GPTs, you need to understand their capabilities and limitations. Here are some tips:

Use GPTs for the right tasks. GPTs are best suited for tasks that require generating text, such as writing articles, creating marketing copy, and translating languages. They are not as good at tasks that require factual accuracy, such as answering questions about complex topics or writing code.

Provide GPTs with as much context as possible. The more context you provide GPTs, the better they will be able to generate the desired output. For example, if you are asking GPTs to write an article about a specific topic, provide them with some background information on the topic as well as some examples of similar articles.

Be specific in your prompts. The more specific you are in your prompts, the better the output will be. For example, instead of asking GPTs to "write a blog post about artificial intelligence," ask them to "write a blog post about the top 10 trends in artificial intelligence in 2023."

Test the generated output. Once GPTs have generated the output, be sure to test it to make sure that it is accurate and meets your needs.

Here are some additional tips for mastering GPTs:

Experiment with different models. There are a variety of different GPT models available, each with its own strengths and weaknesses. Experiment with different models to find the one that works best for your needs.

Use prompts and parameters to control the output. GPTs can be controlled using prompts and parameters. Prompts are used to tell GPTs what to write about, and parameters are used to control the style and tone of the output. Experiment with different prompts and parameters to find the ones that produce the desired output.

Use GPTs in conjunction with other tools. GPTs can be used in conjunction with other tools, such as text editors and machine translation tools, to create even more powerful and versatile applications.

GPTs are powerful tools that can be used for a variety of tasks. By following the tips above, you can master GPTs and use them to achieve your goals.

Here are some examples of how GPTs can be used:

Generate content for websites and blogs. GPTs can be used to generate high-quality content for websites and blogs, such as articles, blog posts, and product descriptions.

Write marketing copy. GPTs can be used to write marketing copy, such as ad copy, product landing pages, and email marketing campaigns.

Translate languages. GPTs can be used to translate languages accurately and efficiently.

Answer questions. GPTs can be used to answer questions in a comprehensive and informative way, even if they are open ended, challenging, or strange.

Generate creative content. GPTs can be used to generate creative content, such as poems, code, scripts, musical pieces, email, letters, etc.

GPTs are versatile tools that can be used for a variety of tasks. By experimenting with different models and parameters, you can discover new ways to use GPTs to achieve your goals.

Chapter 16: Understanding the Capabilities of GPTs

GPTs, or Generative Pre-trained Transformers, are a type of large language model (LLM) that can generate text, translate languages, write different kinds of creative content, and answer your questions in an informative way. GPTs are trained on massive datasets of text and code, which allows them to learn the patterns and relationships between words and phrases. This allows them to generate text that is both coherent and informative.

Here are some of the capabilities of GPTs:

Text generation: GPTs can be used to generate text of any length, from a few words to a full-length novel. They can be used to generate different creative text formats of text content, like poems, code, scripts, musical pieces, email, letters, etc.

Translation: GPTs can be used to translate text from one language to another. They are able to accurately translate text between over 250 languages, including English, French, Spanish, German, Chinese, Japanese, and Korean.

Creative writing: GPTs can be used to generate creative writing, such as poems, stories, and scripts. They can also be used to generate new ideas for creative projects.

Question answering: GPTs can be used to answer questions in a comprehensive and informative way. They are able to access and process information from the real world through Google Search and keep their response consistent with search results.

GPTs are still under development, but they have already been used to create a variety of innovative products and services. For example, GPTs have been used to develop chatbots that can have realistic conversations with humans, to generate personalized marketing copy, and to create new educational tools.

Here are some examples of how GPTs are being used today:

- Google Search: GPTs are used to help Google Search provide more relevant and informative results.
- Google Translate: GPTs are used to help Google Translate provide more accurate and natural-sounding translations.

- Bard: Bard is a large language model from Google AI, trained on a massive dataset of text and code. It can generate text, translate languages, write different kinds of creative content, and answer your questions in an informative way.
- ChatGPT: ChatGPT is a large language model chatbot developed by OpenAI. It can generate realistic and coherent chat conversations.
- MuseNet: MuseNet is a large language model from Google AI, trained on a massive dataset of musical scores. It can generate new music and melodies.

GPTs are a powerful new tool that has the potential to revolutionize the way we interact with computers and information. By understanding their capabilities, you can discover new ways to use GPTs to achieve your goals.

Chapter 17: Creating Custom ChatGPT Models

To create a custom ChatGPT model, you will need to:

1.Collect a dataset of text and code. The dataset should be relevant to the task that you want your ChatGPT model to perform. For example, if you want to create a ChatGPT model that can generate marketing copy, you would need to collect a dataset of marketing copy.

2.Preprocess the dataset. This may involve cleaning the data, removing outliers, and converting the data to a format that is compatible with ChatGPT.

3.Train the ChatGPT model. This can be done using a variety of tools and frameworks, such as OpenAI Gym and TensorFlow.

4.Evaluate the ChatGPT model. Once the model is trained, you need to evaluate its performance on a held-out test set. This will help you to identify any areas where the model needs improvement.

5.Deploy the ChatGPT model. Once the model is evaluated and ready for use, you need to deploy it so that it can be used to generate text or perform other tasks.

Here are some additional tips for creating custom ChatGPT models:

- Use a large and diverse dataset. The larger and more diverse the dataset, the better the performance of your ChatGPT model will be.
- Use a powerful GPU. ChatGPT training can be computationally expensive, so it is important to use a powerful GPU to speed up the training process.
- Use a pre-trained model. You can use a pre-trained ChatGPT model as a starting point for your own custom model. This can save you time and effort, and it can also improve the performance of your model.
- Tune the model parameters. You can tune the parameters of your ChatGPT model to improve its performance on specific tasks.
- Monitor the model performance. It is important to monitor the performance of your ChatGPT model over time to ensure that it is still performing well.

Creating custom ChatGPT models can be challenging, but it is also a rewarding experience. By following the tips above, you can create custom ChatGPT models that can be used to solve a variety of real-world problems.

Here are some examples of how custom ChatGPT models can be used:

- Generate marketing copy. ChatGPT models can be used to generate personalized and engaging marketing copy for a variety of products and services.
- Write creative content. ChatGPT models can be used to write creative content, such as poems, stories, and scripts. They can also be used to generate new ideas for creative projects.
- Develop chatbots. ChatGPT models can be used to develop chatbots that can have more natural and engaging conversations with humans.
- Improve machine translation. ChatGPT models can be used to improve the accuracy and fluency of machine translation systems.
- Generate educational content. ChatGPT models can be used to generate educational content, such as textbooks, articles, and lessons.

Custom ChatGPT models have the potential to revolutionize a variety of industries. By understanding how to create and use custom ChatGPT models, you can position yourself to be at the forefront of this exciting new technology.

Chapter 18: Troubleshooting and Optimizing GPTs

Here are some tips for troubleshooting and optimizing GPTs:

Troubleshooting

If GPTs are not generating the desired output:

Make sure that you are using the appropriate model. GPTs are trained on different datasets and use different algorithms, so it is important to choose the right model for your task.

Provide GPTs with as much context as possible. The more context you provide, the better GPTs will be able to understand your intent and generate the desired output.

Be specific in your prompts. The more specific you are, the better GPTs will be able to understand what you want them to do.

Use the right parameters. GPTs have a number of parameters that can be adjusted to control the output. Experiment with different parameters to find what works best for you.

Use a larger and more diverse dataset. If you are using a custom ChatGPT model, make sure that you are using a large and diverse dataset to train it.

If GPTs are generating incorrect or misleading information:

Be aware of the limitations of GPTs. GPTs are large language models, but they are not perfect. They can sometimes generate incorrect or misleading information, especially if they are not trained on a high-quality dataset.

Always fact-check the information that GPTs generate.

If GPTs are slow:

Use a more powerful GPU. GPTs are computationally expensive, so using a more powerful GPU can improve their performance.

Use a cloud-based platform. If you do not have access to a powerful GPU, you can use a cloud-based platform to access GPTs.

Use a smaller model. GPTs are available in a variety of sizes. If you need to improve performance, you can use a smaller model.

Optimizing

Use the right model: Choose the model that is most appropriate for your task. Consider the size of the model, the dataset it was trained on, and the algorithms it uses.

Provide context: Provide GPTs with as much context as possible. This will help them to understand your intent and generate the desired output.

Be specific in your prompts: The more specific you are in your prompts, the better GPTs will be able to understand what you want them to do.

Use the right parameters: Experiment with different parameters to find what works best for you.

Use a large and diverse dataset: If you are using a custom ChatGPT model, make sure that you are using a large and diverse dataset to train it.

Use a powerful GPU: GPTs are computationally expensive, so using a more powerful GPU can improve their performance.

Use a cloud-based platform: If you do not have access to a powerful GPU, you can use a cloud-based platform to access GPTs.

Use a smaller model: GPTs are available in a variety of sizes. If you need to improve performance, you can use a smaller model.

By following these tips, you can troubleshoot and optimize GPTs to improve their accuracy and performance.

Here are some additional tips for troubleshooting and optimizing GPTs:

Check the documentation: The documentation for GPTs is a great resource for troubleshooting and optimization tips.

Ask for help: There is a large and active community of GPT users. If you are having trouble, you can ask for help on the forums or on social media.

GPTs are powerful tools that can be used for a variety of tasks. By troubleshooting and optimizing them, you can get the most out of these tools.

Part 6: Mastering the Assistants API

The Assistants API is a powerful tool that allows you to build and integrate voice assistants into your products and services. To master the Assistants API, you need to understand its capabilities and limitations.

Capabilities

The Assistants API allows you to:

Create and manage custom voice assistants

Integrate custom voice assistants into your products and services

Access pre-trained voice assistants, such as Google Assistant and Amazon Alexa

Customize the behavior of voice assistants

Get insights into how voice assistants are being used

Limitations

The Assistants API is still under development, so there are some limitations to keep in mind:

Not all features are available for all voice assistants

Some features may require additional configuration or development

The Assistants API may not be compatible with all products and services

How to Master the Assistants API

To master the Assistants API, you need to:

- Understand the basics of voice assistants. How do voice assistants work? What are the different types of voice assistants? What are the benefits of using voice assistants?
- Learn about the Assistants API. What are the different features of the Assistants API? How do you use the Assistants API to create and manage custom voice assistants? How do you integrate custom voice assistants into your products and services?
- Experiment with the Assistants API. The best way to learn is by doing. Experiment with different features and see what works best for you.
- Read the documentation. The Assistants API documentation is a great resource for learning about the different features of the API and how to use them.
- Ask for help. There is a large and active community of Assistants API users. If you are having trouble, you can ask for help on the forums or on social media.

Here are some additional tips for mastering the Assistants API:

- Start small. Don't try to build a complex voice assistant right away. Start with a simple task, such as creating a voice assistant that can answer basic questions.
- Use pre-trained voice assistants. Pre-trained voice assistants, such as Google Assistant and Amazon Alexa, already have a lot of functionality built in. You can use

pre-trained voice assistants as a starting point for your own custom voice assistants.

- Customize the behavior of voice assistants. You can customize the behavior of voice assistants to meet your specific needs. For example, you can change the voice of the voice assistant, add new features, or change the way the voice assistant responds to certain prompts.

Get insights into how voice assistants are being used. The Assistants API provides insights into how voice assistants are being used. This information can help you to improve your voice assistants and make them more useful for your users.

Benefits of Mastering the Assistants API

There are many benefits to mastering the Assistants API, including:

- Improved user experience: Voice assistants can provide a more natural and engaging user experience than traditional interfaces.
- Increased productivity: Voice assistants can help users to be more productive by automating tasks and providing information quickly and easily.
- New opportunities: The Assistants API can open up new opportunities for businesses and developers to create innovative products and services.

Chapter 19: Understanding the Capabilities of the Assistants API

The Assistants API is a powerful tool that allows you to build and integrate voice assistants into your products and services. It has a wide range of capabilities, including:

- Creating and managing custom voice assistants: You can use the Assistants API to create custom voice assistants that are tailored to the specific needs of your product or service.

- Integrating custom voice assistants into your products and services: You can integrate custom voice assistants into your products and services using a variety of methods, such as through web services, SDKs, and device integrations.

- Accessing pre-trained voice assistants: You can also use the Assistants API to access pre-trained voice assistants, such as Google Assistant and Amazon Alexa. This allows you to add voice assistant functionality to your products and services without having to build your own voice assistant.

- Customizing the behavior of voice assistants: You can customize the behavior of voice assistants to meet your specific needs. For example, you can change the voice of the voice assistant, add new features, or change the way the voice assistant responds to certain prompts.

- Getting insights into how voice assistants are being used: The Assistants API provides insights into how voice assistants are being used. This information can help you to improve your voice assistants and make them more useful for your users.

Here are some specific examples of what you can do with the Assistants API:

- Create a voice assistant that can answer questions about your product or service.
- Create a voice assistant that can control smart home devices.
- Create a voice assistant that can help users to be more productive by automating tasks and providing information quickly and easily.
- Integrate a voice assistant into your existing website or app.
- Develop a new product or service that is powered by a voice assistant.

The possibilities are endless! With the Assistants API, you can create voice assistants that can do anything you can imagine.

Benefits of Understanding the Capabilities of the Assistants API

There are many benefits to understanding the capabilities of the Assistants API, including:

- Improved user experience: Voice assistants can provide a more natural and engaging user experience than traditional interfaces.

- Increased productivity: Voice assistants can help users to be more productive by automating tasks and providing information quickly and easily.
- New opportunities: The Assistants API can open up new opportunities for businesses and developers to create innovative products and services.

By understanding the capabilities of the Assistants API, you can start to think about how you can use voice assistants to improve your products and services, and create new experiences for your users.

Chapter 20: Building Agent-Like Experiences with the Assistants API

To build agent-like experiences with the Assistants API, you need to understand the following concepts:

What is an agent-like experience? An agent-like experience is one in which the user interacts with a voice assistant in a way that is similar to interacting with a human agent. For example, an agent-like voice assistant would be able to understand the user's context, respond to open ended questions, and complete tasks in a conversational way.

What features of the Assistants API are relevant to building agent-like experiences? The Assistants API provides a number of features that can be used to build agent-like experiences, including:

- Context awareness: The Assistants API can provide voice assistants with access to the user's context, such as their location, device, and previous interactions. This can help voice assistants to generate more relevant and informative responses.

- Natural language processing (NLP): The Assistants API provides voice assistants with access to powerful NLP capabilities. This allows voice assistants to understand the user's intent, even when the user's requests are open ended or ambiguous.
- Dialog management: The Assistants API provides voice assistants with dialog management capabilities. This allows voice assistants to maintain a conversation with the user and complete tasks in a conversational way.

How to Build Agent-Like Experiences with the Assistants API

To build agent-like experiences with the Assistants API, you can follow these steps:

1.Design the agent-like experience: What tasks do you want the voice assistant to be able to complete? How should the voice assistant interact with the user?

2.Choose the right voice assistant: The Assistants API supports a variety of pre-trained voice assistants, as well as custom voice assistants. Choose the voice assistant that is most appropriate for your needs.

3.Develop the voice assistant: If you are using a custom voice assistant, you will need to develop it using the Assistants API. This involves training the voice assistant on a dataset of text and code, and developing dialog flows to handle the different tasks that the voice assistant will be able to complete.

4.Integrate the voice assistant into your product or service: The Assistants API provides a variety of ways to integrate voice assistants into products and services. You can integrate voice assistants using web services, SDKs, and device integrations.

5.Test and deploy the agent-like experience: Once you have developed and integrated the voice assistant, you need to test it thoroughly and deploy it to your users.

Tips for Building Agent-Like Experiences with the Assistants API

Here are some tips for building agent-like experiences with the Assistants API:

- Use context awareness: Use the Assistants API's context awareness features to provide the voice assistant with as much context as possible. This will help the voice assistant to generate more relevant and informative responses.
- Use natural language processing: Use the Assistants API's NLP capabilities to allow the voice assistant to understand the user's intent, even when the user's requests are open ended or ambiguous.
- Use dialog management: Use the Assistants API's dialog management capabilities to allow the voice assistant to maintain a conversation with the user and complete tasks in a conversational way.
- Design for conversations: Think about how the voice assistant will interact with the user throughout the entire conversation. Make sure that the voice assistant is able to understand the user's context, respond to open ended

questions, and complete tasks in a way that is natural and engaging.

- Test and iterate: Once you have developed a prototype, test it thoroughly with users and get feedback. This will help you to identify areas where the agent-like experience can be improved.

By following these tips, you can build agent-like experiences with the Assistants API that are informative, engaging, and helpful to your users.

Chapter 21: Troubleshooting and Optimizing the Assistants API

To troubleshoot and optimize the Assistants API, you can follow these steps:

Troubleshooting the Assistants API

If you are having problems with the Assistants API, you can troubleshoot the issue by following these steps:

1.Check the documentation: The Assistants API documentation is a great resource for troubleshooting problems. It provides detailed information on how to use the API and how to resolve common errors.

2.Check the logs: The Assistants API logs can provide you with information about what went wrong and why. Check the logs for any errors or warnings.

3.Try to reproduce the issue: If you are able to reproduce the issue, you can provide more information to the support team.

This will help them to identify the cause of the problem and resolve it more quickly.

4.Contact support: If you are still having problems, you can contact the Assistants API support team. They will be able to help you troubleshoot the issue and resolve it as quickly as possible.

Optimizing the Assistants API

There are a number of things you can do to optimize the Assistants API, including:

- Use the right voice assistant: The Assistants API supports a variety of pre-trained voice assistants, as well as custom voice assistants. Choose the voice assistant that is most appropriate for your needs.
- Optimize your dialog flows: Make sure that your dialog flows are efficient and effective. Avoid unnecessary loops and branches.
- Use caching: You can cache the results of common requests to improve the performance of your voice assistant.
- Use a scalable architecture: If you are expecting a large number of users, you need to design your architecture to be scalable.
- Monitor your usage: Monitor your usage of the Assistants API to identify any areas where you can optimize your usage.

Tips for Troubleshooting and Optimizing the Assistants API

Here are some additional tips for troubleshooting and optimizing the Assistants API:

- Use a consistent development environment: When developing your voice assistant, use a consistent development environment. This will help you to identify and resolve problems more easily.
- Test your voice assistant thoroughly: Before deploying your voice assistant to production, test it thoroughly with users. This will help you to identify any problems and resolve them before they impact your users.
- Keep your voice assistant up to date: The Assistants API is constantly being updated with new features and bug fixes. Make sure that your voice assistant is up to date to take advantage of the latest features and bug fixes.
- Monitor your voice assistant after deployment: Even after you have deployed your voice assistant, continue to monitor it to identify any problems. This will help you to ensure that your voice assistant is always performing at its best.

By following these tips, you can troubleshoot and optimize the Assistants API to build reliable and performant voice assistants.

Part 7: Advanced Applications of OpenAI's Products

OpenAI's products, such as GPT-3 and DALL-E 2, are powerful tools that can be used for a variety of advanced applications, including:

- Creative writing: GPT-3 and DALL-E 2 can be used to generate creative text formats, such as poems, code, scripts, musical pieces, email, letters, etc., as well as images, videos, and other creative content.
- Translation: GPT-3 can be used to translate text between over 250 languages accurately and efficiently.
- Code generation: GPT-3 can be used to generate code in a variety of programming languages, such as Python, JavaScript, and C++.
- Fact-checking: GPT-3 can be used to fact-check information by comparing it to a variety of sources, including news articles, scientific papers, and government websites.
- Question answering: GPT-3 can be used to answer questions in a comprehensive and informative way, even if they are open ended, challenging, or strange.
- Education: GPT-3 and DALL-E 2 can be used to create personalized educational materials and experiences for students of all ages.
- Research: GPT-3 and DALL-E 2 can be used to generate new hypotheses, design experiments, and analyze data.

- Product development: GPT-3 and DALL-E 2 can be used to generate new product ideas, create prototypes, and test products with users.

Here are some specific examples of how OpenAI's products are being used for advanced applications today:

- Google Search: GPT-3 is used to help Google Search provide more relevant and informative results.
- Google Translate: GPT-3 is used to help Google Translate provide more accurate and fluent translations.
- Bard: Bard is a large language model from Google AI, trained on a massive dataset of text and code. It can generate text, translate languages, write different kinds of creative content, and answer your questions in an informative way. Bard is powered by GPT-3.
- ChatGPT: ChatGPT is a large language model chatbot developed by OpenAI. It can generate realistic and coherent chat conversations. ChatGPT is also powered by GPT-3.
- MuseNet: MuseNet is a large language model from Google AI, trained on a massive dataset of musical scores. It can generate new music and melodies. MuseNet is also powered by GPT-3.
- DALL-E 2: DALL-E 2 is a text-to-image diffusion model created by OpenAI. It can generate realistic images from text descriptions. DALL-E 2 is still under development, but it has the potential to revolutionize the way we create and consume visual content.

OpenAI's products are still under development, but they are already being used to create innovative products and services that are changing the world. As these products continue to develop and become more powerful, we can expect to see even more advanced and innovative applications emerge.

Chapter 22: Using OpenAI's Products for Creative Writing

OpenAI's products, such as GPT-3 and DALL-E 2, can be used for creative writing in a variety of ways. Here are some examples:

Generating text in different formats

GPT-3 can be used to generate text in a variety of formats, such as poems, code, scripts, musical pieces, email, letters, etc. This can be useful for writers who want to experiment with different genres or styles of writing.

Brainstorming ideas

GPT-3 can be used to brainstorm ideas for new stories, characters, or plots. This can be helpful for writers who are struggling to come up with new ideas or who are stuck on a particular project.

Developing characters

GPT-3 can be used to develop characters by generating backstory, dialogue, and descriptions. This can be helpful for writers who want to create more complex and believable characters.

Generating plot points

GPT-3 can be used to generate plot points for stories. This can be helpful for writers who want to create more suspenseful or engaging stories.

Revising and editing work

GPT-3 can be used to revise and edit work by suggesting changes to grammar, spelling, style, and tone. This can be helpful for writers who want to improve their writing skills or who want to get feedback on their work.

Collaborating with other writers

GPT-3 can be used to collaborate with other writers by generating text that is consistent with the other writer's style and tone. This can be helpful for writers who are working on collaborative projects, such as screenplays or novels.

Here are some specific tips for using OpenAI's products for creative writing:

- Be specific in your prompts. The more specific you are in your prompts, the better the output will be. For example, instead of asking GPT-3 to "write a poem," ask it to "write a sonnet about a love that is lost."
- Use the right parameters. GPT-3 has a number of parameters that can be adjusted to control the output. For example, the "temperature" parameter controls the randomness of the output. A higher temperature will produce more creative and original output, but it will also be more likely to produce incorrect or misleading output.

- Use a variety of tools. OpenAI's products can be used in conjunction with other tools, such as text editors and word processors, to create even more powerful and versatile workflows.

Experiment and have fun! The best way to learn how to use OpenAI's products for creative writing is to experiment and have fun. Try different prompts and parameters to see what works best for you.

OpenAI's products are powerful tools that can be used to enhance your creative writing skills and to create new and innovative works of art.

Chapter 23: Using OpenAI's Products for Education and Training

OpenAI's products, such as GPT-3 and DALL-E 2, can be used for education and training in a variety of ways. Here are some examples:

Creating personalized learning experiences

OpenAI's products can be used to create personalized learning experiences for students of all ages. For example, GPT-3 can be used to generate personalized practice problems, create quizzes and tests, and provide feedback to students. DALL-E 2 can be used to generate personalized illustrations and diagrams to help students learn new concepts.

Teaching students to code

OpenAI's products can be used to teach students to code in a variety of programming languages. For example, GPT-3 can be used to generate code examples and to provide feedback to students on their code. DALL-E 2 can be used to generate graphical representations of code, which can help students to understand complex coding concepts.

Training employees

OpenAI's products can be used to train employees on new skills and procedures. For example, GPT-3 can be used to generate training materials, such as presentations and handouts. DALL-E 2 can be used to generate simulations and training scenarios.

Educating the public

OpenAI's products can be used to educate the public on a variety of topics. For example, GPT-3 can be used to generate articles, blog posts, and social media posts about complex topics in a way that is easy to understand. DALL-E 2 can be used to generate infographics and other visual content to help the public learn new concepts.

Here are some specific tips for using OpenAI's products for education and training:

- Be specific in your prompts. The more specific you are in your prompts, the better the output will be. For example, instead of asking GPT-3 to "create a lesson on the water cycle," ask it to "create a lesson for 4th grade students on the water cycle that includes a diagram of the water cycle and a quiz on the different stages of the water cycle."
- Use the right parameters. OpenAI's products have a number of parameters that can be adjusted to control the output. For example, the "temperature" parameter controls the randomness of the output. A higher

temperature will produce more creative and original output, but it will also be more likely to produce incorrect or misleading output.

- Use a variety of tools. OpenAI's products can be used in conjunction with other tools, such as learning management systems (LMSs) and presentation software, to create even more powerful and versatile workflows.

Experiment and have fun! The best way to learn how to use OpenAI's products for education and training is to experiment and have fun. Try different prompts and parameters to see what works best for you and your students or learners.

OpenAI's products are powerful tools that can be used to transform the way we teach and learn. By using OpenAI's products, educators and trainers can create personalized, engaging, and effective learning experiences for students and learners of all ages.

Chapter 24: Using OpenAI's Products for Business and Productivity

OpenAI's products, such as GPT-3 and DALL-E 2, can be used for business and productivity in a variety of ways. Here are some examples:

Generating marketing copy

GPT-3 can be used to generate personalized and engaging marketing copy for a variety of products and services. For example, GPT-3 can be used to generate ad copy, product descriptions, and email marketing campaigns.

Writing product reviews

GPT-3 can be used to write product reviews that are informative and helpful to consumers. GPT-3 can access and process information from the real world through Google Search and keep its response consistent with search results. This allows GPT-3 to generate product reviews that are accurate and up-to-date.

Creating customer support chatbots

GPT-3 can be used to create customer support chatbots that can have realistic and helpful conversations with customers. GPT-3 can answer customer questions, resolve customer issues, and provide support to customers in a timely and efficient manner.

Generating leads

GPT-3 can be used to generate leads for businesses by generating personalized outreach emails and social media posts. GPT-3 can also be used to create landing pages and other marketing materials that are designed to convert visitors into leads.

Automating tasks

GPT-3 can be used to automate a variety of tasks, such as data entry, scheduling meetings, and generating reports. This can free up employees' time to focus on more strategic and value-added tasks.

Improving decision-making

GPT-3 can be used to improve decision-making by providing businesses with insights and recommendations based on data. GPT-3 can also be used to generate scenarios and simulations to help businesses make more informed decisions.

Here are some specific tips for using OpenAI's products for business and productivity:

- Be specific in your prompts. The more specific you are in your prompts, the better the output will be. For example, instead of asking GPT-3 to "write a marketing email," ask it to "write a marketing email for a new product launch that is targeted to small business owners in the United States."
- Use the right parameters. OpenAI's products have a number of parameters that can be adjusted to control the output. For example, the "temperature" parameter controls the randomness of the output. A higher temperature will produce more creative and original output, but it will also be more likely to produce incorrect or misleading output.
- Use a variety of tools. OpenAI's products can be used in conjunction with other tools, such as CRM systems and marketing automation platforms, to create even more powerful and versatile workflows.
- Experiment and have fun! The best way to learn how to use OpenAI's products for business and productivity is to experiment and have fun. Try different prompts and parameters to see what works best for you and your business.

OpenAI's products are powerful tools that can be used to transform the way we work. By using OpenAI's products, businesses can improve their productivity, efficiency, and profitability.

Part 8: The Future of OpenAI and AI

The future of OpenAI and AI is very exciting. The technology has already come a long way, and it continues to develop at a rapid pace. It is impossible to say for sure what the future holds, but it is clear that AI has the potential to revolutionize many industries and aspects of our lives.

OpenAI is at the forefront of AI research and development, and its products are already having a significant impact on the world. As AI continues to develop, OpenAI is well-positioned to play a leading role in shaping the future of this technology.

It is important to note that AI is a powerful tool, and it can be used for both good and evil. It is up to us to ensure that AI is developed and used responsibly. If we do so, AI has the potential to make the world a better place.

Here are some of the key challenges that we need to address as we move forward with AI:

Ensuring that AI is used for good: We need to develop safeguards to ensure that AI is not used to harm people.

Ensuring that AI is fair and equitable: We need to ensure that AI does not discriminate against any group of people.

Ensuring that AI is transparent and accountable: We need to be able to understand how AI systems work and to hold them accountable for their actions.

If we can address these challenges, AI has the potential to make the world a better place for everyone.

Chapter 25: The Future of OpenAI's Products

The future of OpenAI and AI is very promising. OpenAI is at the forefront of AI research and development, and its products, such as GPT-3 and DALL-E 2, are already having a significant impact on the world.

As AI continues to develop, OpenAI is well-positioned to play a leading role in shaping the future of this technology. Here are some specific predictions for the future of OpenAI and AI:

OpenAI will continue to develop and release new and more powerful AI models. These models will be able to perform a wider range of tasks and generate more creative and original content.

OpenAI's products will be used to create new and innovative products and services. For example, OpenAI's products could be used to create personalized educational experiences, realistic virtual assistants, and immersive video games.

OpenAI's products will democratize creativity. OpenAI's products will make it possible for anyone to be creative, regardless of their skills or experience. This will lead to a more diverse and inclusive creative landscape.

OpenAI's products will challenge the way we think about the world. OpenAI's products will force us to rethink the way we think about intelligence, creativity, and the nature of reality.

Overall, the future of OpenAI and AI is very bright. OpenAI is well-positioned to play a leading role in shaping the future of this technology, and its products have the potential to revolutionize many industries and aspects of our lives.

Here are some specific examples of how OpenAI's products could be used in the future:

Personalized education: OpenAI's products could be used to create personalized educational experiences for students of all ages. GPT-3 could generate personalized learning plans, practice problems, and feedback for each student. DALL-E 2 could generate images, diagrams, and other visual aids to help students learn complex concepts.

Virtual assistants: OpenAI's products could be used to create realistic virtual assistants that can understand and respond to human language in a natural way. These virtual assistants could be used to provide customer support, answer questions, and even help people with creative tasks.

Video games: OpenAI's products could be used to create immersive video games that are indistinguishable from reality. GPT-3 could generate dialogue, storylines, and other creative content for the game. DALL-E 2 could generate realistic images and environments for the game.

These are just a few examples of the many ways that OpenAI's products could be used in the future. As AI continues to develop, we can expect to see even more innovative and transformative applications emerge.

Chapter 26: The Broader Impact of AI on Society

Artificial intelligence (AI) is having a broad impact on society, both positive and negative.

Positive impacts:

AI can improve the efficiency and effectiveness of many tasks, from manufacturing to healthcare.

AI can automate repetitive and dangerous tasks, freeing up workers to focus on more creative and strategic work.

AI can help us to better understand the world around us and to solve complex problems.

AI can create new products and services that improve our quality of life.

For example, AI is being used to develop new drugs and treatments for diseases, to create personalized educational experiences for students, and to develop self-driving cars that could make transportation safer and more efficient.

Negative impacts:

AI could lead to job displacement, as machines become capable of performing tasks that are currently done by humans.

AI could be used to develop autonomous weapons systems that could kill without human intervention.

AI could be used to create surveillance systems that could track and monitor our every move.

AI could be used to manipulate people and spread misinformation.

For example, AI-powered social media algorithms have been shown to be capable of polarizing people and spreading misinformation. AI-powered facial recognition systems have also been shown to be biased against certain groups of people.

It is important to note that the broader impact of AI on society will depend on how it is developed and used. If AI is developed and used responsibly, it has the potential to make the world a better place. However, if AI is developed and used irresponsibly, it could have negative consequences for society.

Here are some specific things that we can do to ensure that AI is developed and used responsibly:

Invest in research on the ethical and social implications of AI.

Develop international guidelines for the responsible development and use of AI.

Educate the public about the potential benefits and risks of AI.

Support policies that promote the responsible development and use of AI.

By taking these steps, we can help to ensure that AI is used for good and that it benefits all of humanity.

Chapter 27: Conclusion

The future of OpenAI and AI is very exciting. The technology has already come a long way, and it continues to develop at a rapid pace. It is impossible to say for sure what the future holds, but it is clear that AI has the potential to revolutionize many industries and aspects of our lives.

OpenAI is at the forefront of AI research and development, and its products are already having a significant impact on the world. As AI continues to develop, OpenAI is well-positioned to play a leading role in shaping the future of this technology.

It is important to note that AI is a powerful tool, and it can be used for both good and evil. It is up to us to ensure that AI is developed and used responsibly. If we do so, AI has the potential to make the world a better place.

Here are some of the key challenges that we need to address as we move forward with AI:

Ensuring that AI is used for good: We need to develop safeguards to ensure that AI is not used to harm people.

Ensuring that AI is fair and equitable: We need to ensure that AI does not discriminate against any group of people.

Ensuring that AI is transparent and accountable: We need to be able to understand how AI systems work and to hold them accountable for their actions.

If we can address these challenges, AI has the potential to make the world a better place for everyone.

Printed in Great Britain
by Amazon